LEKTÜRE ENGLISCH

Liam Cleary

Echoes and Other Short Stories

für die Mittelstufe

W0339120

STARK

Bildnachweis
Umschlag: © ZEFA/Heilmann
S. 4: Hans Reinhard, Eiterbach;
S. 19: http://fcit.coedu.ust.edu/holocaust/gallery.htm;
S. 20, S. 24 und S. 26: http://www.ushmm.org/olympics/zcd065b.htm;
S. 32: Erhard Schwambach und Erhard Pausegrau: Südafrika. München, Bruckmann 1995, S. 139; S. 48: ae-Dokumentation;
S. 61: David Rose.

ISBN: 3-89449-356-9

© 1998 by Stark Verlagsgesellschaft mbH
D-85318 Freising · Postfach 1852 · Tel. (0 81 61) 1790
u 05-01
Nachdruck verboten!

Inhalt

Autor: Liam Cleary

Vorwort

Liebe Schülerinnen, liebe Schüler,

"Echoes" entstand über einen langen Zeitraum hinweg. Als ich die Arbeit daran abschloss, hatte ich in meinen Geschichten einen weiten Weg zurückgelegt. Die 'Reise' führte mich nach British Columbia in Kanada, nach Amerika, Irland, Berlin, London und Südafrika. Im Laufe meiner Arbeit an "Echoes" nahm ich an einer Gerichtsverhandlung gegen einen Mörder teil und erfuhr, wie das Rotkehlchen zu seinem Namen kam. Ich machte sogar einen Ausflug in die Vergangenheit, in eine Zeit, als das Leben noch ganz anders war als heute. Ich besuchte die Olympischen Spiele von Berlin im Jahre 1936, als Jesse Owens berühmt wurde und stieß auf die vergessenen Helden der ersten Atlantiküberquerung im Flugzeug.

Aber in all diesen Geschichten steckt weit mehr als ich euch in ein paar Worten erzählen kann. Daher ist es nun an euch, mehr herauszufinden!

Wie ihr sicher wisst, ist das Lesen englischer Geschichten eine tolle Gelegenheit, etwas über die Welt zu erfahren und gleichzeitig eure Sprachkenntnisse zu verbessern. Damit ihr nicht ständig im Wörterbuch nachschlagen müsst, habe ich die schwierigeren Wörter auf Deutsch erklärt.

Und nun viel Spaß beim Lesen. Enjoy yourselves!

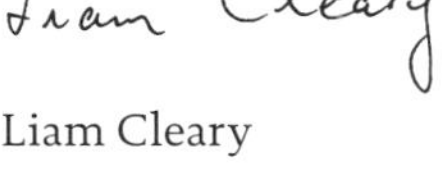

Liam Cleary

Echoes

To be honest with you there are times I'm glad I've no children. I wouldn't swop[1] with my sister in Bellingham for all the money in the world. She's four years younger than I am and much prettier too but she looks about five years older than I do. That's not to say I don't want children, I do. Just not like hers; they're loud and bad-mannered[2]. Actually, now that I mention Bellingham that reminds me: I shouldn't have been anywhere near the wildlife station when the call came in from Vaseux Lake that Tuesday afternoon. I should have been on vacation in Bellingham. We had it all planned. I'd mind her kids while she took a break. The week before however, Jeff Kennedy, my boss, asked me to switch holidays with him so he could take his wife on a long weekend to Seattle. He'd forgotten it was his wife's birthday.

"You don't mind, do you Karen?"

What could I say? I could see he was in a bit of domestic trouble[3]. Besides, ever since I started at the wildlife station Jeff's been good to me. He showed me the ropes[4] at the start; how to care for the birds, how to band[5] them, what to feed them. He explained the paperwork that had to be done, that sort of thing. Then when Tony, my boyfriend, broke off[6] with me two weeks after asking me to marry him, Jeff was very understanding. He asked if I was okay, if I wanted to take a

---

1 *to swop* – tauschen
2 *bad-mannered* – ungezogen, unhöflich
3 *domestic trouble* – häusliche Auseinandersetzungen
4 *to show s.o. the ropes* – jmdn. in alles einweihen
5 *to band* – beringen
6 *to brake off* – mit jmdm. Schluss machen

few days off. I felt I owed him a favour[7]. So I reported for work while he showed his wife around Seattle. "The bird's badly injured" the young voice said, "can you come right away?" I threw my gear[8] in the jeep and headed off.

***

Wildlife Operator Karen Kingston put the keys in her pocket and got out of the jeep. The waters of Vaseux Lake lapped[9] softly in the background. The campsite was quiet. She could see a few children playing baseball, a young couple walking a collie dog, a white-haired lady reading a book. There was none of the mad chaos of a peak-season[10] Saturday in July. A short distance away Karen spotted a man standing beside a young girl. Walking towards them, she could see that the girl was holding something under her arm.

"Thank you for coming, my name is Declan Waverman and this is my daughter Kelly. She found the chickadee[11] over there by the rocks", said the tall, well-spoken man. The daughter, who had red hair and looked about twelve or thirteen, spoke up: "I think its wing might be broken. Will it be okay? Can I keep it?"

"Hi there, Kelly. I'm Karen. Let's have a look at what you've got. Why don't you bring the bird over to my jeep?" At the jeep Karen carefully examined the bird as Mr Waverman explained that he and his daughter had spent the past two nights camping by the shores of Lake Vaseux. Kelly had found

---

7 *to owe s.o. a favour* – jmdm. einen Gefallen schulden
8 *gear* – Sachen
9 *to lap* – plätschern
10 *peak-season* – Hochsaison
11 *chickadee* – Meise

the bird lying injured and unable to fly.

"She asked me if she could phone you."

"You sure did the right thing", said Karen. "But this is no chickadee. It's a stray swift[12]. A white-throated[13] swift to be exact. A female too. I don't think we've banded one around here before.

They are very common in the North-West of the US. Swifts nest in dark crevices[14] high up on cliffs that are very hard to reach. You'll sometimes see them here catching insects in the sky. It looks as if this one has lost its way. Could be a hatch-year bird."

"What's that?" asked Kelly

"That means it was born earlier this year. We may be the first people she's ever seen." The swift had tiny eyes and every now and then it moved its head. "It doesn't seem frightened of you at all", Karen continued. "The wing's not broken but the poor bird is exhausted. I don't know if she'll survive. Sometimes they never fly again. I think I'd better get her back to the station."

At this news a shadow of disappointment passed across Kelly's face. "I'd love to keep her."

"I know that, but you see Kelly I have to band the bird. More importantly she needs food, warmth and rest. She'll get that over at the wildlife station where I work. When she's stronger we'll see if she wants to fly again. How long more are you planning to stay?"

Mr Waverman looked at her daughter. "I have to be back in the city for a business meeting next Monday afternoon. Maybe we could call by your station to see how the bird is doing before we head home."

---

12 *stray swift* – streunender Mauersegler
13 *white-throated* – weißkehlig
14 *crevice* – Spalte

"Sure. We're open at eight. How's that?"

"That's fine. Can I give you my number? You can ring us on the mobile phone if there are any developments. It was very good of you to come so quickly."

"That's my job, Mr Waverman", Karen replied, taking his business card from him. "Well, I'd better get back to the station. 'Bye now."

Kelly stroked[15] the swift's neck gently with one finger, whispered "goodbye" and watched Karen Kingston drive away with the bird.

***

15 *to stroke* – streicheln

I suppose I'll never really know why Tony got cold feet[16]. He seemed so certain when he asked me to marry him. So much in love with me. Down on Clinton's Bridge one evening in late June it was. I was completely happy. We told my Dad, my Mom, all our friends. Afterwards, after he changed his mind I mean, I cried for a week. The worst bit was Dad's reaction. It was as if I'd done something wrong. As if it was all my fault. Tony and I had talked about building a house, about me giving up my job at the wildlife station, having kids, all the usual stuff. He knew I wanted to have children. Babies always remind me of the young chics I see day after day at work; beautiful, so tiny and cute. In need of loads of food, attention, love. I still remember the joy that rushed through me the day I first held a young sparrow[17] in my hands and fed it.

***

Later in the week Kelly and her father visited an old university friend of his who lived nearby. Returning to the campsite, Kelly was quieter that ever.

"You're thinking about the swift aren't you?"

Kelly nodded[18].

"How about if we drive over there tomorrow and see how it's doing."

"Oh, yes please, yippee!"

Her father laughed. "Only if you agree to build our campfire tonight."

---

16 *to get cold feet* – kalte Füße (= Angst) bekommen
17 *sparrow* – Spatz
18 *to nod* – nicken

"I promise! I promise!"

Kelly kept her promise and that evening they sat around the fire, talking. As darkness began to fall they sang a song or two but Declan Waverman could see his daughter's mind was a few short miles away.

"I'm sure the people at the wildlife station will look after the swift better than we could".

"I wasn't thinking about that"

"What then?"

"Do I have to spend next weekend with Mom?"

"Yes, you do. What put that into your head?"

"And Christmas, too?"

"Yes, and Christmas too."

"Oh please, Dad, not Christmas. I hated it last year. She brought that stupid new boyfriend of hers."

"I know, I know. But we've discussed this already. You have to spend a certain amount of time with her. You know that. Your mother loves you as much as I do."

"Why did she leave then?"

On receiving no answer, Kelly turned away from her father and pretended to sleep. The sound of lakewater drifted up[19] from the shoreline[20].

***

I was worried. The swift was getting no better. Each day, morning and evening, I'd go out to the outhouse and swat[21] some flies. She was barely able to eat them. On Thursday evening I banded the bird and took her to the cliffs. Holding

---

19 *to drift up* – heraufwehen
20 *shoreline* – Wasserlinie, Uferlinie
21 *to swat* – totschlagen

her in my hands, I launched[22] her into the air. Seconds later she dropped, helpless and frightened, at my feet. Back at the station I got Jeff to examine her.

"Don't look too good, Karen, this one's not gonna make it if you ask me."

Before I went home that evening I fed her a few more flies. As I set her down to sleep the swift's body felt cold and shivery[23]. A bad sign. When I got home I sat on the front porch listening to the sun go down. It's a favourite pastime of mine: listening to the songs of the bird change, then quieten until eventually I'm there in the twilight with only one or two songs still to be heard. If I'm in a good mood I sing the last birds to sleep. Sometimes though I think of the day I came back from the doctor's. The words I said, the look on Tony's face, the way he let go off my shoulder and looked into the distance. "The doctor thinks it'd be dangerous to have kids. There could be complications." By the time I said "She wants to carry out a few more tests." I don't think he was even listening.

***

On Friday the door of the wildlife station opened and in walked Declan and Kelly Waverman.

"Hi! I wasn't expecting you until Monday."

"We were wondering how the swift is" Declan said smiling and looking in Kelly's direction. "Can I see her?", Kelly asked.

"Sure you can", laughed Karen, but it doesn't look too good. I tried to launch her yesterday and though she's been eating a little she seemed as weak as ever."

---

22 *to launch* – hier: werfen
23 *shivery* – frösteln

While Kelly talked to the swift, Karen Kingston showed Declan around the station.

"She loves nature. I promised her a holiday for her birthday. There was only one holiday she wanted; a camping holiday! Personally-speaking I'd give anything to sleep in a real bed for a change", said Declan with a smile, rubbing the stiff muscles of his neck. They laughed at this. There was something kind about him that Karen liked.

"Kelly reminds me of myself when I was her age. Birds, animals, fresh air. My father never allowed us to keep pets so I spent ages in the woods".

"I often think her interest in nature is her way of escaping the fact that her mother no longer lives with us."

"Could be. But she's at the age when she wants to be exploring the world and finding new interests. She's found a good hobby. I wouldn't worry too much if I were you."

As the Wavermans were leaving the station, Kelly looked at the bird and said "I wish I could be her mother and hold her forever in my arms, warm and tight like a baby. Then she'd get better."

***

It was the craziest thing I'd ever done. Jeff thought so too but reckoned we had nothing to lose. All the way back to the house I kept hearing my father's voice "She's with the birds." My father used to say that whenever my mother did something totally crazy. When I pulled back the bedcovers and climbed into bed I laughed aloud at what I was doing. My hands were shaped in the form of a cup. I moved down in the bed and spilled[24] the swift softly on to my stomach. After

24 *to spill* – verschütten

switching off the bedside light, I lay in the darkness as the young bird moved around on my belly. It was the strangest experience, like an echo from deep down inside me.

As my body grew warmer I felt the bird move slowly upwards and lie under my chin. The soft feathers of her wings tickled from time to time but I didn't dare laugh for fear of frightening her. At last the swift moved to my armpit and settled down to sleep. It was about the darkest, warmest place the bird could have found. Then we slept. At five thirty in the morning I woke when the swift stirred[25]. For the first time in almost a week the bird felt truly warm. I lay there for ages talking in whispers[26] to it. Later I lifted it from the bed and we had breakfast together! Coffee and cereal for me. A feast[27] of flies for her! She ate eagerly. Then she chirped[28], loudly. The sweetest chirping sound you can imagine. The first chirp since Kelly had found her!

I knew the Wavermans were due to leave early the next morning so I rang Declan and asked if I could come over. An hour later the three of us met at the campsite. Kelly was all eyes[29], jumping up and down with excitement as I showed her the swift. I described how I'd put her idea to work, taken the bird home with me. Here we have one quite healthy swift" I said. All it needed was a Mom! "The only problem is", I went on, "I'm not sure what do with her."

"How do you mean?"

"Well, either we get her to fly again or someone has to mind her. Seeing as you found her I thought perhaps you'd like to keep her."

---

25 *to stir* – bewegen
26 *whisper* – Geflüster
27 *feast* – Festmahl
28 *to chirp* – zwitschern
29 *to be all eyes* – genau beobachten

We both looked at Kelly, waiting for her answer. Slowly, she began to speak:

"I'd like that but she wouldn't be free with me back home in Vancouver. I think we should give her the chance to decide for herself what she wants to do. Maybe to find her own mother and father or to join other swifts. But if she can't fly then I'd love to look after her.

"A very sensible answer young lady. Now let's see if she'll fly."

We drove to the cliffs. The wind was gusting[30] and away in the distance we could see and hear many other birds crossing the skies. Circling, swooping[31], calling out. Kelly lifted the swift gently from the box. Holding the bird in her hands she walked forward a few steps. The swift looked alive and alert[32], as if it knew exactly what was happening. I watched Kelly open her palms and stretch her arms to the sky as I had told her to do. The swift sprang outwards and up and free. Up and up it climbed, skybound[33], flying now as well as it had done the day it strayed too far from home and got lost. The three of us cheered and danced around and clapped our hands in applause as our little friend disappeared from view.

***

That's three months ago now. There are times I'm glad I've no children. Honestly. I wouldn't swop with my sister in Bellingham for all the money in the world. But I often

---

30 *to gust* – stürmisch wehen
31 *to swoap* – herabstoßen
32 *alert* – aufmerksam, aufgeweckt
33 *skybound* – Richtung Himmel, himmelwärts

wonder about the swift, where she is now. And Kelly too; how she's getting on. Which reminds me, I found that card the other day. Where did I put it? I'd love to talk to her.

The Origin of the Robin

There was once an old Indian who had an only son, a boy called Iadilla. Iadilla's father was very ambitious and had great hopes for his son. He prayed that one day his son would become a warrior[1] or a chieftain[2]. Now it is a traditional part of every young Indian's life that at a certain age he must fast[3] for many days. He does this so that he may gain a guardian spirit[4] who will walk with him on his long path through life. The boy Iadilla had now reached this age. His father decided the boy should fast longer than any of those Indians who were famous for their wisdom and power as chieftains or for their strength and bravery as warriors. He did this in the hope that Iadilla would be better than all the other Indians in the tribe. One morning he took Iadilla to one side and said:

"You must do as I tell you, my son."

His father told him how he was to prepare for the fast: "Each day you must go to the sacred sweat-lodge[5] and bath. This will make you pure. Then you will be ready to meet your guardian spirit. You must fast like a man. Do not fear. You will not be alone. I will be with you. During your fast I promise I will visit you each day. At the end of the twelve days I will bring you food and my blessing[6]."

The boy listened to every word his father said and because he loved his father dearly he did everything he had been told

---

1 *warrior* – Krieger
2 *chieftain* – Häuptling
3 *to fast* – fasten
4 *guardian spirit* – Schutzengel
5 *sweat-lodge* – Schwitzhütte
6 *blessing* – gute Wünsche

to do. Finally, when his father thought the time had come for him to begin, Iadilla lay down in a small lodge, closed his eyes and waited for the spirit to visit him. Morning after morning his father came, telling him to be strong. Each day he reminded Iadilla of the wisdom and strength that would be his after he had passed this great test. The boy never said a word in reply until the ninth morning. Shortly after the sun had risen his father appeared at the door, his dark shadow filling the room:

"Father", Iadialla began, "I've seen this night the most evil dreams. No good will come of my fast they tell me. They tell me I should stop now while I have the chance, before it is too late. May I end it now and return at another time?"

"My son you know not what you say. There are but three nights left for you to fast. Three nights between you and great glory. If you stop now all glory will leave you like sand falling through your fingers or leaves blown by the wind. Will you not grant your old father his greatest wish: to see his son Iadilla become a great warrior or a star among chieftains?"

The son promised to try harder. He covered his eyes more closely to shut out the light that had caused him to want to end his fast. He forced his mind and body to try and finish the final three days of the fast. However, on the eleventh day he fell weak again. Again he asked his father if he might break his fast and begin it at another time. The father gave Iadilla the same answer as before. Then he promised Iadilla he would go and prepare the boy's first meal for the next day. When the boy moaned[7] his father asked angrily: "Will you cause shame and sorrow[8] to fall upon your father now that his sun is setting in the west?" Iadilla promised he would not and lay still and barely breathing at his father's feet.

---

7 *to moan* – stöhnen

8 *sorrow* – Trauer

The next day Iadilla's father got up a few minutes before dawn[9]. He put his son's breakfast in a basket. Delighted that Iadilla had done as he had wished, he hurried to the lodge. When he arrived there he was astonished to hear Iadilla talking to himself. Longing to know what was being said, he peered[10] though a small opening in the hut. The sight he saw and the words he heard would stay with him for the rest of his days. Iadilla's breast was covered with vermillion[11] and the boy was just finishing the painting of his shoulders and breast.

"My father would not listen to me. He pushed my limbs beyond their strength. He has ruined my future but it is he who has lost. It is he who shall be lonely, not I. I shall be forever happy in my new shape for I have shown obedience and respect to my parent. My guardian spirit has not given me all that I wanted but he has shown pity on me in a different way. Now the time has come. I must go."

On hearing this, terror gripped the old man's heart and he burst into the lodge crying out: "My son I beg you, do not betray[12] me, do not leave your aging father."

However, before his father could stop him, Iadilla flew with the quickness of a bird to the top of the lodge and landed easily on the highest pole. There and then, for the first time, his father noticed the boy had changed into a beautiful small bird with a red breast.

"Do not be sad, my father. The change your eyes now see means I shall be happy in my new shape, happier than ever I could have been as a man. I shall be happy and at peace even though I shall never be the brave warrior and wise chieftain

---

9 *dawn* – Sonnenaufgang
10 *to peer* – schauen
11 *vermillion* – zinnoberrot
12 *to betray* – verraten

you so wished me to become. I shall remain a friend to all men and women and shall live near the houses where they live. I shall find food on the mountain sides, by rivers and in the fields. My path in life is the bright clean air and you shall know how greatly this pleases me. To lift the heavy stone of sadness from your breast I will sing you songs each day of your life. I am free now from all the tears life can bring."

And before the old man could say a single word of farewell to his son Iadilla, the young robin[13], delighted with the gift of wings, flew high into the air and off towards a neighbouring wood. And that is how the bird we call the robin came to be.

---

13 *robin* – Rotkehlchen

A Hand in Friendship

The stadium fell quiet. You could almost hear a pin[1] drop. Down below in the sports arena the qualifying round of the long jump was in progress[2]. All eyes were fixed on one athlete for whom the moment of truth was coming closer and closer. The year was 1936. The man everybody at the Berlin Olympic Games was watching was an American Negro by the name of Jesse Owens. I don't think I realized the full importance of the events I was watching then. How could I have? I was only 12 when my father took me to the Games. But I remember it well, as if it was only yesterday. Usually we recall unhappy, tragic days best of all. Like where we were or what we were doing the day war broke out, the day Kennedy was shot, the day the Berlin Wall was begun. But this was a day to remember for good reasons. A day that lives on in our memory for the joy that goes with it. I see the excited look on my father's face, on all the faces around me. I see the flags, the huge crowds of people. I can still hear the roars[3] and the waves of applause ...

***

That was Berlin, the 1930s. Hitler and the Nazis had just come to power. Times were hard. In 1929 the Wall Street Crash had shaken the world and left millions unemployed in

---

1 *pin* – Stecknadel
2 *progress* – im Gange
3 *roars* – die Schreie

every country. Germany was no different. Many of the fathers in our street had no work. Many of the families in our street had very little to eat. People were worried. About the prospect of no work, no money, no food. About the talk of war growing louder and louder in our ears. Our family was a bit luckier than most. My father had a good job but I still don't know how he managed to get tickets for the Games. In 1931 the IOC, the International Olympic Committee, had selected Berlin ahead of Barcelona as their choice for the 1936 Games. The German Organizing Committee held its first meeting in Berlin on the 24 January 1933. A week later Hitler became German Chancellor. In the months and years that followed, the question of the Berlin Olympics grew more and more controversial. Sir Eric Phipps, the British ambassador in Berlin warned his government that Hitler was planning the Games as a political event. That the Berlin Olympics was a wonderful propaganda opportunity the Nazi government was determined[4] to use ...

Even before the Games started there was trouble in the air. Mainly because of the Jews. Hitler didn't want any Jews to take part. Eventually the German committee agreed that Jews from other countries could take part. Then they finally said that German Jews would also be allowed to compete. I think they were afraid of world reaction. In America there was a strong campaign to stop the US Olympic team from going to Berlin. 43 per cent of those Americans questioned thought a boycott was a good idea. In the end the US Olympic Committee chairman, a man called Avery Brundage, made sure the US team went to Berlin. He believed the Olympic movement should not be part of the fight between Jews and Nazis. "The Games must go on" he would later say at the Munich Olympics and that was his attitude in 1936 too.

---

4 *to determine* – entschließen

CA
SC

***

That first morning my father knocked on the door of my bedroom. It was very early and I was only half-awake. I heard him say “I have a surprise for you, Kurt! Get dressed! We’re going to the Games.” I couldn’t believe my ears. For a couple of sleepy-eyed seconds I didn’t react. “Come on,” he laughed, “don’t you want to go?” Then it hit me. I jumped out of bed and pulled on my trousers. My mother saw us off. Before long we were heading for the stadium. So it was thanks to Avery Brundage and my father that I came to be watching Jesse Owens and all the other American athletes at the 1936 Berlin Games.

***

The opening ceremony is something I will never forget. 4,000 athletes had come to take part in all the different events. I saw the Italian and French teams coming round in the parade. My father pointed out all the athletes he knew to me. We watched them give the Nazi salute and walk on. The crowd applauded loudly. Then came the British. I noticed that the British team never saluted when they went past. I asked my father why not but he just shrugged[5] his shoulders and said nothing. Later I learned that many of the athletes and the teams were unsure whether they should give the Nazi salute. If the International Olympic Committee itself was divided about the Berlin Olympics then I suppose it's no surprise that the athletes had their problems too. I can hear the trumpets blowing as the Olympic flag is raised. I see the runner running round the arena with a torch in his hand. I can picture the Olympic flame burning. And men in uniforms standing beneath flags with great black swastikas ...

The Games were a huge success in many ways. Everything was well organized. The city was transformed; the streets were cleaned and specially decorated with Olympic and Nazi flags, all anti-Jewish posters were taken down, the buildings were beautifully done up, banned[6] foreign newspapers could be bought in many shops, it was a wonderful time. And everything went according to[7] the government's plan. Everything that is except for one thing: Jesse Owens became the name that everyone remembers when thinking of the Berlin Games. Yet what many people do not know, or have simply forgotten, is that his story is the story of two men not one.

Jesse Owens was born in Danville, Alabama in 1913. His full name was James Cleveland Owens. He was the son of a

---

5 *to shrug* – Achselnzucken
6 *to ban* – verbieten
7 *according to* – nach

poor farm worker and the grandson of a slave. When Jesse was about nine the whole family moved to Ohio. In Junior High School he started running very fast times on the track. In 1933 he won three events in the Interscholastic Championships in Chicago. In Ohio State University he became a star, an outstanding[8] athlete who broke record after record. At one meeting he set three world records and equalled[9] a fourth. By the time he arrived in Berlin he was perhaps the best athlete of his day. One man stood between him and the long jump Gold medal. A white-skinned, sandy-haired[10] German athlete called Carl Ludwig 'Luz' Long. In the run-up[11] to the Games Luz Long was said to have jumped over 26 feet. The American and British athletes weren't quite sure about this because the German government made it hard to get any information on their athletes. Hitler wanted blonde, white-skinned German athletes to prove[12] his theories correct by winning Gold Medals at the Games and he was prepared to help them do that in whatever way he could.

***

I remember the cheering of the crowd on the day of the long jump. The long jump athletes were quite close to me. My father lifted me up every time they came over towards us to start their run. Luz Long was my hero. With his first jump he broke the Olympic record. He was famous for starting well in competitions and now he'd done it again. We cheered and

---

8 *outstanding* – hervorragend
9 *to equal* – erreichen
10 *sandy-haired* – rotblond
11 *run-up* – Vorbereitungszeit
12 *to prove* – beweisen

clapped and hats flew up in the air. When Owens came over towards us I watched him closely. He looked so strong and powerful. I remember a news reporter speaking to Owens. It seems the reporter asked him "Has Hitler walked out on you?" Owens looked up to where Hitler had been sitting while the other athletes were jumping. The Chancellor's seat was empty. Hitler had left.

Owens himself has described the emotions he felt at that moment: "I looked over to where the German ruler had been sitting. No one was in his box. A minute ago he had been there. Besides, he'd already snubbed[13] me by refusing the Olympic Committee's request to have me sit in that box. I could add two and two. This was too much. I was mad, hate-mad, and it made feel wild. I was going to show him. He'd hear about this jump, even if he wouldn't see it! I felt the energy coming into my legs ... I began my run ... Finally, I ran faster and faster until I was moving almost as fast as I did when I ran the hundred-yard dash[14]. Suddenly the foul board[15] was in front of me. I hit it, went up high ... I heard the referee shout "Foul!" I had run too fast ... I had been thinking too hard about setting a record and not enough about form. I'd gone half a foot over the foul board ... My second jump was not good. But I didn't foul. I didn't go far enough to qualify. I had one jump left ... I looked around nervously, panic creeping[16] into every cell of my body. On my right was Hitler's box. It was empty. This was his way of saying I was a member of an inferior race who would give an inferior performance."[17]

---

13 *to snub* – jmdn. brüskieren
14 *hundred-yard dash* – 100-Meter-Lauf
15 *foul board* – Absprungbrett beim Weitsprung
16 *to creep* – kriechen; hier: jmdn. überkommen
17 All quotes from: Jesse Owens: An American Sports Hero by Thomas Kral, Washington D.C.

Watching Jesse Owens that day I had no idea of what was going through his mind. Nor the huge pressure he was under. Reading his words all these years later explains a lot of things to me. At one stage in the competition Luz Long walked over to Owens. It was just before Owens's last jump. If Owens fouled he would be disqualified and that would make Long the clear favourite to win the final. If Owens tried to make sure he didn't foul he wouldn't jump far enough to qualify. It needed to be a perfect jump. After a while it seemed to me that the two men were talking to one another. That surprised me. I tugged[18] the sleeve[19] of my father's coat and pointed across to where the two athletes were standing. He looked

18 *to tug* – zerren, ziehen
19 *sleeve* – Ärmel

and nodded and I remember my father saying to me "I wonder what language they are speaking: German or English?" I sat back in my seat. The crowd fell silent again. And waited and watched. Owens started his run. The tension[20] was incredible. He took off like a bird and qualified by more than a foot. We would all have to come back for the final to see which of them was the best.

The day of the final I got up at daybreak. We prepared food to take with us and this time my mother came along. We got to the stadium quite early. After a few hours the finals began. We watched Owens win the hundred meters in 10.3 seconds. He was really fast. He followed this victory with a Gold medal in the 200 meters. Then the American relay team, of which Owens was a member, also took Gold. He now had three medals. I asked my father if Luz would be able to beat Owens. I got no answer. I think many people knew that Jesse Owens was a special athlete with special talents. At last the long jump final started. Our hopes were raised when Luz broke his own record. And he broke the Olympic record. But Owens went one better. The Gold medal was going to the black man from Alabama and there was nothing we could do about it. Hitler, who refused to shake hands with Owens, could not hide his anger. He was furious.

I went home that evening a little disappointed yet tremendously[21] excited by what I had seen. Lying in bed at night, my head was full of the fantastic events I had watched. I couldn't sleep. My mother came in and talked to me. After a while I turned over and dropped off to sleep. What I didn't know was that as I lay in my bed Long and Owens were spending the evening talking to one another in the Olympic village. They spoke about their families, their sport, the Games, the

---

20 *tension* – Spannung
21 *tremendous* – ungeheuer, über alle Maßen

future for both of them after they retired[22] from athletics. What kind of job they would look for. How hard it would be to live without sport. They wondered whether the war that everybody was talking about would really come. And if it came what it would mean for them. They promised to write to one another, to keep in touch, to build on the friendship they had made. The way Owens put it later was that they "didn't make the mistake of not seeing past each other's skin colour to what was within."

***

The war the two men so greatly feared – the Second World War – did come. And Germany and America were on opposing sides. Luz Long died in that war, somewhere in Africa. Unlike my father, he never came home to his wife and family. In the years before Long died he started writing letters to Jesse Owens. He described how he had had to join the German army and leave his wife and son. He was very unsure about what he was doing. More than anything else however, he was worried about what his family would do if he did not return from the war. Yet he couldn't leave the army for fear of what would happen to his loved ones back home.

Jesse Owens returned to America and found little had changed because of his Gold medals. He was a black man and still had to ride in the back of the bus. As he himself said "I wasn't invited to shake hands with Hitler, but I was not invited to the White House to shake hands with the President either." He found work as a playground janitor[23]. Life was tough for him and for a while he got nowhere. Then

22 *to retire* – in Pension gehen
23 *janitor* – Hausmeister

he became a disc jockey. After that he went into business and built up a public relations firm[24]. Many years later he went on goodwill visits to India and other countries. He visited schools and was very involved in sports at High School level.

***

The years passed. I went to work in America. I settled down[25], got married, started a family. That's a good while ago now. Then, one day, Jesse Owens came to our local school. The newspaper I worked for sent me to cover his visit. The children knew his name and that one of America's most famous athletes was coming to talk to them. Yet somehow I felt he meant far more to me than to any of those boys or girls. It was then I discovered what the two men had said to each other the day of the qualifying round of the long jump. Their friendship started just before Owens's third and final jump. Owens was becoming more and more nervous as the pressure increased with each bad jump he made. Then Hitler walked out of the stadium in an attempt[26] to unsettle[27] the American champion.

It was just after the German leader left that one of the fairest sporting moments in Olympic history took place. Luz Long went over to Owens, put his hand on the black man's arm and introduced himself. He asked why Owens was jumping so badly. He wanted to know if it was because Hitler had walked out. Owens wasn't sure what to say to this so he gave no answer. Long could see exactly what the problem

---

24 *public relations firm* – Firma für Öffentlichkeitsarbeit
25 *to settle down* – sesshaft werden
26 *attempt* – Versuch
27 *to unsettle* – durcheinander bringen

was. He told Owens to change his run-up a little and to relax. Owens laughed out loud. Long said he'd like to talk to him when the competition was over. In broken English he told him he 'need not fear to foul'.

The way Owens described it those schoolchildren it was as if all the tension poured instantly out of him. 'Like a cloud-burst[28]' was the way he put it. He knew then he would qualify. That explained a great deal of what I had seen back in 1936. The two men had been discussing the number of steps Jesse Owens needed to take to make a perfect jump! Long did all this with the man who was his greatest rival for the sporting medal he himself hoped to win. I have often thought about that moment and the courage[29] it took to do that. Especially in a stadium in which most of the 100,000 people there wanted Long to win. I find myself thinking about it more and more nowadays. Most of all I think about it when I see fewer and fewer examples of fair play in sport. Everyone wants to be a winner, at any price and by any means[30]. Luz Long, the hero of my childhood, has remained a hero of mine throughout my adult life.

***

Luz Long's last letter to Jesse Owens was written in 1939. Fearing that he might die in the war, Long asked his "only friend outside Germany" to visit his wife and son after the war. He was afraid he said that he might "die for the wrong thing. But whatever might become of me, I hope only that my wife and son will stay alive." "Tell them," Long wrote, "why I

---

28 *cloudburst* – Wolkenbruch
29 *courage* – Mut
30 *by any means* – mit jedem Mittel

had to do this and how the good times between us were". Which is exactly what Owens did. The friendship between Luz and Jesse grew into one between Jesse and Luz's son Karl. The hand of friendship that had first been offered in 1936 at the Berlin Games stretched on into further generations.

I passed the Children's Hospital and continued on. To my right, whenever I looked, I could see the Indian Ocean and the Bay of Plenty. The traffic was slow but I'd given myself enough time to get where I was going. To do what I had to do.

"I have a speaking engagement[1] at noon, mother, and a business meeting after that. I won't be over to see you until this evening", I had said a few hours earlier.

My mother believes every word I tell her and the older she gets the fewer awkward[2] questions she asks. Whenever something goes wrong I keep my reasons for being late or not turning up at all vague and general. What she doesn't know can't hurt her: that's my motto. I slowed to a halt to let a father and his two children cross the road. In the sticky late-morning heat I longed for the comfort of the air-conditioned station wagon I normally drive. While I waited I read the names of the curry dishes at an Indian food stall[3]. They were written in big, black letters on round white signs: Special Fish Masala[4], Special Curry Masala, Special Madras Masala, Atomic Bomb.

Arriving at the hotel I parked the car nearby and got out. The radio was still on. A news report about a speech the President, P. W. Botha[5], had given uptown. I listened to the

---

1 *speaking engagement* – Vortrag
2 *awkward* – hier: peinlich, schwierig
3 *food stall* – Imbiss-Stand
4 *Masala* – ein Gericht
5 *P. W. Botha* – Weißer Politiker in Südafrika. Er war der letzte weiße politische Führer, der versuchte, das Apartheid-System in Südafrika zu erhalten.

mechanical sound of his words, ticking away:

"... South Africa's problems will be solved by South Africans not by foreigners ... We will not be forced into doing what we don't want to do. To those who prefer revolution to reform, I say they will not succeed ..."

Reaching in through the side window I turned off the applause. The day, like all the days that summer in Durban, was incredibly warm. The weathermen were forecasting thunder and lightning. I rolled down the sleeves of my white shirt and straightened my tie.

Across the road the two hands of a large clock dithered[6] between twenty-six minutes and twenty-five minutes to twelve. The Head of Security Police and his party of close friends would be sitting down to dinner about now. I didn't want to be late. Or early. It was never good to leave too much

6 *to dither* – schwanken

time for questions. Get in, do the business, get out. The lights beyond the tower on the opposite side of the road had been smashed in. A tall, white-gloved policeman was giving orders, keeping the traffic moving. Every now and then a car horn honked[7] loudly, its driver in a rush to get away. Could anything be worse than being stuck in a traffic-jam on a main street in Durban at this hour of the day, at this time of the year? There was a light breeze blowing in from the harbour. Standing there, I caught the distinctive smell of rubber still burning from the night before. Twenty yards away, a beggar[8] standing outside a bottle store was watching me. He walked over and shoved a dirty black hand under my face. "Get out of here" I shouted. He threw me a faceful of hate and wandered off.

I opened the boot[9], took out my jacket and put it on. Then I lifted out the black briefcase. The boot closed at the second attempt. The lock had been vandalized the previous week and needed fixing. The briefcase felt heavier than the last time I'd picked it up. I walked towards the doors of the hotel. My soft white hands were sweaty and tight. Blasted[10] heat! All I could think of was the swim I would have in the pool when I got home. When it was all over. The security guard greeted me with a second-hand smile. He'd been standing at the exact same spot when I drove by the night before. I smiled back and flashed my card. I was a senior steel consultant[11]. At least that's what the card said. The name didn't interest him. He was going off duty[12] at noon.

---

7 *to honk* – hupen
8 *beggar* – Bettler
9 *boot* – Kofferraum
10 *blasted* – verdammt
11 *consultant* – Berater
12 *off duty* – dienstfrei

Two plain clothes police officers were standing in the foyer. I had a bell boy[13] lead me past them to the restaurant. It was small and intimate, more crowded than I expected. These were the 'reasonable' South Africans Botha had spoken of the day before: the ones who would not accept the one-man one-vote system. A fan whirred[14] above my head as I stood in the doorway. My watch said 11.42. In one corner, on the right-hand side of the room, the nine people I had come for were standing around a large, long dinner table. It had been reserved for them. I knew them to be policemen, magistrates, politicians. Their body language said a lot. They were all facing the Head of Police. He was a tall man of about fifty, with sharp eyes and a thin smile. Each of the men had a glass of whiskey or beer in one hand. They were in fine spirits. Most of them were joking and laughing, having the time of their lives. By the sound of them they'd been drinking for a while. They began taking their places.

I moved in their direction looking for the nearest, most suitable table. There wasn't a single one free. Of the two tables closest to them one was covered in booklets, leaflets, brochures. The other had a big goldlettered Reserved sign on it. To sit down there would be asking for trouble. I turned away. Directly across from them, at the window, I spotted a vacant table for two. It wasn't ideal but it would do. I walked towards it, making my way skillfully between the tables. The beautiful, expensive tablecloths caught my eye. I noticed the knives, forks and other items of cutlery[15], the napkins, the flowers, the candle on each table, the ivory[16] ashtrays, the

---

13 *bell boy* – Hotelboy, Hotelpage
14 *to whirr* – surren
15 *cutlery* – Besteck
16 *ivory* – Elfenbein

chandelier[17]. All perfectly in place, everything where it should be. The hotels and restaurants of my childhood had all been like this one. Elegant, opulent, exclusive.

My right arm was as stiff as a poker[18]. I could sense my pulse beating, my brain concentrating, my fingers trembling. When I reached the other side of the room I sat slowly down and placed the briefcase carefully at the leg of the table. I draped my jacket across the back of the chair.

"Hello Sir, would you care to order?"

The waitress who had come over was holding a tray in her right hand. She was tall and had lovely brown eyes. Her long black hair was tied up at the back. I guessed she was about twenty.

"Could I see the menu first?" I asked.

"Certainly, Sir."

She went away to get me one. I watched her as she went. She had strong, smooth legs. The seconds seemed to be racing by. Eventually, the old lady at the table next to me leaned over and gave me her menu. She had the kind of blue rinse[19] in her hair my grandmother used to have and she looked out at me through bifocal glasses.

"Here you are," she said to me, "I don't need it any longer. They can be terribly slow in here. Sometimes I think they don't want to serve us. I recommend the duck a la orange" she said with a glint[20] in her eye.

I smiled. "Thanks ever so much" I replied. I looked beyond her, across to where the Head of Police was sitting. He seemed to be telling a joke. His companions were hanging on every word he said. Using the flame of the candle in front of

---

17 *chandelier* – Kronleuchter
18 *poker* – Schüreisen
19 *rinse* – Haartönung
20 *glint* – Schimmer

me I lit a cigarette and pretended to study the menu. I wasn't a bit hungry. It was 11.47.

My thoughts kept returning to the briefcase close to my right foot. I laid the menu down and studied the people around me. I could just about catch pieces of conversations in progress, some in English, some in Afrikaans; a young girl in the middle of the room was complaining she didn't want sauce with her chicken, an army major dressed in a ridiculous[21] uniform was going on about a war he'd fought in back in the good old days. I glanced at my watch again; 11.49. It was time to get out. To get as far away as possible.

The head waiter passed by, muttering to himself about something or other. I turned to take my jacket from the back of the chair. Just as I was about to rise, I heard a soft voice from behind me say "Here's the menu, Sir."

For a moment I was caught for words.

"Oh yes, lovely, thank you."

I took it from her even though I had one already. She seemed nervous. As if she had something unpleasant to do. The fingers of her slender[22] left hand were fiddling with the buckle[23] on her watchstrap. She had a very good figure. In other circumstances I might have flirted with her and asked her name or what time she was getting off work. It would have been no problem. I've always had a way with women. I'd have invited her for coffee or offered to buy her an ice-cream. Not a drink mind you. She didn't look the type to be impressed by hotels or restaurants.

"And, I've been asked to remind you that this is a no-smoking area."

---

21 *ridiculous* – lächerlich
22 *slender* – schlank, schmal
23 *buckle* – Schnalle

The sharpness of her voice was unexpected. I wasn't sure how to react. In the street outside a car horn started honking wildly, blindly. Like Botha and those last words of his before I'd turned the radio off: "... we will not, we will not give in to outside demands ..."

Suddenly, through the window, I saw the black beggar I'd shouted at earlier. He hadn't gone away, the fool. He was standing on the pavement[24] outside with his back to me, one hand in the pocket of his dirty trousers, the other outstretched. He was no more than ten feet away. He hadn't a hope. A great roar of vulgar laughter shot across from the far side of the room. Without looking at the girl I stubbed out[25] my cigarette. Ringlets of smoke swirled[26] up between us. "I'm terribly sorry" I heard myself say.

---

24 *pavement* – Gehsteig
25 *to stub out* – ausdrücken
26 *to swirl* – wirbeln, umherwirbeln

"Why not America?"

In the words of Charles Lindbergh it was "the Everest of aviation", the most difficult flight in the world at that time. And the three men standing around the tiny, one-engined Junkers W 33 'Bremen' parked at Baldonnell airport in Ireland were about to undertake[1] it; yet another attempt[2] to be the first successful East to West transatlantic flight. It was the 12th of April, 1928. Their aim was to fly from Ireland to the coast of North America. Into the strong Atlantic winds. Something nobody had ever done. Four attempts in the past 15 months had all failed. But for the Germans Hermann Köhl and Günter Freiherr von Hünefeld and for Irishman James Fitzpatrick this only added to the excitement.

Köhl and von Hünefeld had themselves made a previous[3] attempt. So too had Fitzmaurice. Both times bad weather put an end to their trips. Ever since the Wright brothers had got their plane off the ground in North Carolina on December 17, 1903, men and women were not only dreaming of conquering[4] the skies like Icarus and others had done centuries before, they were actually doing something about it. In 1927, travelling in the opposite direction, Lindbergh had flown himself and his single-engined monoplane The Spirit of St Louis into the record books. Overnight he became the most famous man in the world.

---

1 *to undertake* – unternehmen
2 *attempt* – Versuch
3 *previous* – vorherig
4 *to conquer* – erobern

In Ireland the news of the flight of the 'Bremen' was of great interest to the general public. The heartbreak of the Civil War was still fresh in everybody's minds and an adventure story was just what the people needed to cheer them up. Day after day the crew waited patiently for good weather and day after day the excitement grew. Many people in Ireland thought the three men were foolish, others believed them to be very brave. But no matter what people thought of them one thing was certain: everybody was excited by the whole project.

***

The story begins in March, 1928. Having put a significant[5] amount of money into the unsuccessful[6] first attempt, sponsors of a flight to America are becoming hard to find. Famous sponsors such as the Hearsts withdraw their support. It is now that the fundraising[7] talents of von Hünefeld help get the project started. He speaks to businessmen in Bremen who are looking for publicity for their town. They become interested in his idea and agree to help him. He manages to raise enough money to buy the 'Bremen'. Preparations for a flight begin.

***

---

5 *significant* – bedeutend
6 *unsuccessful* – erfolglos
7 *fundraising: to raise funds* – Geld einwerben

The frustration of having a dream but not being able to make it come true is something James Fitzmaurice understood well. He had flown in the war and was well qualified as a pilot. His ambition to fly the Atlantic could just as easily have come to nothing but for a bit of luck and the help of his German companions. His sister May recalls the type of person her brother was:

MAY FITZMAURICE: My brother was a man before his time. He used to have terrific schemes. But it wasn't easy. People didn't always believe him. They thought he was a dreamer, a bit mad perhaps. You know in those days to even think about flying across the Atlantic was shocking and most certainly frightening. Then there was the problem of finding money. Lack[8] of funds was always a problem. He often got impatient with people who didn't see things his way. But somehow I felt that one day, maybe, he'd see his dream come true. That's what we all hoped and prayed for because we knew it was something very important to him ...

March 26, 1928: The aircraft leaves Berlin and flies to Ireland. For two weeks the Atlantic weather battering[9] the West coast of Ireland makes any take-off impossible.

If we look back to the year 1928 it is very hard to imagine the difficulties the three men and their team of engineers faced at that time. We are used to sitting into powerful planes and travelling to America in a short period of time. We also take radar, satelites and other technological developments as a normal, everyday part of life. The only time we stop to think about the amazing achievements[10] man has made in the aviation world is when something goes seriously wrong. But that is not how it was then. For von Hünefeld, Fitzmaurice

---

8 *lack* – Mangel
9 *to batter* – schlagen
10 *achievement* – Leistung, Errungenschaft

and Köhl flying such a long distance was not easy as aviation expert Conor Keating explains:

CONOR KEATING: The problem was that airplanes long ago were very underpowered and this one of course was overloaded. It sounds strange to be overloaded with only 600 hundred gallons[11] of fuel but everything depends on the size of the plane and for that aircraft, which was only five and a half tons in weight, that was a massive load. They had to make the airfield in Baldonnell longer by one field to help them take off. The plane hardly climbed at all after take-off. The operation was only barely possible and it all depended on such factors as a few pounds of extra fuel or a few revolutions on the engine. The difference between success and failure was very small. They lived with the fear of failure. And they knew how dangerous it was too. After flying in the Second World War they knew that the plane would burn like a torch[12] if it forcelanded[13] with that much fuel on board[14]. For the three men on board good preparations were all important. They had to have the plane ready and as light as possible. So they did everything they could; they got the airplane into perfect condition. They had mechanics with them who had come over from Germany. Everything was tuned up[15]. They tried to stop icing by putting oil on the outside skin of the plane and then they left out everything they possibly could to get the weight down. They took no radio because it would have been too heavy. That meant they had no contact to the outside world. They were completely alone. It was a real test of character and skill.

---

11 *gallon* – Gallone
12 *torch* – Fackel
13 *forceland* – zur Landung zwingen
14 *board* – an Bord
15 *to tune up* – tunen

For many people who knew the three-man crew it was a worrying time. May Fitzmaurice was one of those people who had to wait and pray that all would go well:

MAY FITZMAURICE: The stress before and during the flight was very real. I remember travelling on the trams, hearing people talking. Everybody thought James was so foolhardy[16]. In the weeks before the flight I would listen to the people as they talked about his reponsibilities, about his wife and small child and how he could even think about risking his life and his family's future. But I was always confident he would succeed. He was so keen[17], so very, very keen to go on some flight like that.

Alan Doyle was a boy at the time of the flight of the Bremen. His father was interested in airplanes and gave his young son a love of flying that lasted all his life:

ALAN DOYLE: We went out to the airfield before the flight. The plane was standing there and we were allowed look into it. It was a great thrill[18] just to be able to look into it. I still see two big tanks. I didn't know what they were but they were behind the cockpit. And on the far side there was a very thin black cushion on a seat. There was another seat hanging on the wall behind. And that's where Baron von Hünefeld sat. He was an extraordinary looking man. I don't think he took any notice of us. He was a very aloof[19] individual and he wore a monocle too.

Many friendships were made before and during the flight of the Bremen. Not only did the crew become good friends but the technicians and mechanics became close also. One such mechanic who enjoyed this experience was Irishman

---

16 *foolhardy* – tollkühn
17 *keen* – begeistert, eifrig, stark interessiert
18 *thrill* – Erregung, ein richtiges Erlebnis
19 *aloof* – unnahbar

Johnny Maher. He worked with the German mechanics who came from Germany to help get the plane ready.

JOHNNY MAHER: When we went outside it was a beautiful night. One of the two German mechanics said to me "Johnny, you say the pilot's good. I know the engine is good because I work on the engine. The airframe is good because I work on the airframe. Now the Irish weather is good. Why not America?" His English wasn't perfect but he and his friend were very good mechanics and I always remember those words "Why not America?" That was the spirit of the time. You were always afraid something might go wrong and that we would never see them again. But their determination and spirit was greater than the fear they felt.

***

April 12, 1928. Weather good. At 5.38 a.m. the Bremen begins its take-off. The three men set off to try and conquer this Everest of the air. When asked many years later what he recalled of the flight James Fitzmaurice had the following to say:

JAMES FITZMAURICE: We had a very small little airplane. We had enough fuel for about forty hours flying. At the moment of take-off we had the whole of the Irish Cabinet out there to see us safely into the air. We were very worried about the take-off but we had a certain amount of confidence in the aircraft that we were flying and we just battled through[20]. And we did get safely into the air. Once we got off the ground I was confident we would do it, something nobody had ever done before. The start was the hardest bit.

---

20 *to battle through* – sich durchkämpfen

April 12, 1928. 7.05 a.m.: The Bremen is seen for the last time over Irish soil, flying in a north-westerly direction. The airplane covers the first 175 kilometers in 1 hour and 27 minutes at a speed of 121 km per hour. Alan Doyle recalls the early stage of their flight quite clearly:

ALAN DOYLE: They had a comfortable flight for the first few hours. Everything went beautifully, the engine worked perfectly, the weather was good, and suddenly they saw this huge bank of cloud straight ahead of them. Now that would mean they were going to fly into bad weather; wind and ice and everything else. They soon ran into a tremendous storm and fog. This made flying far more difficult and was a great test for the crew. They had to change their altitude from time to time. Sometimes they went down as low as 15 metres above sea level.

April 12, 1928. 12.00 p.m.: The Bremen is now some 1,500 km from Baldonnell.

As time passed it became clear to James Fitzmaurice that the early part of the flight had gone well. For him it was now a case of keeping going and praying that luck was on their side.

JAMES FITZMAURICE: As darkness fell we soon realized that what we thought was a mountain range was an extremely dangerous jet black cloud bank reaching way up to above 20,000 feet and clearly of the ice-forming type. We climbed to 6,000 feet and continued flying in a westerly direction, rocked by the force of the storm we had entered. It was pitch[21] dark. We were reduced to instrument flying and it fast turned into a nightmare. Hour followed hour with no sign of the storm ending.

To a modern pilot and aviation expert like Conor Keating it seems incredible that the men tried an Atlantic crossing with the instruments they had:

---

21 *pitch* – pechdunkel

CONOR KEATING: Their plane was unlike modern aircraft in that it had very few instruments. The art of blind flying as it was called then was very new. They had an air speed indicator[22], a compass and they had of course an altimeter[23] to tell them the altitude at which they were flying over either the land or the sea. They didn't have any radio navigation aids because such things didn't exist. Such machines hadn't been invented by then. They also had difficulty in keeping their own attitude[24] while flying in cloud and this was to be very important during the flight. Modern aircraft have an instrument called the artificial horizon[25] and by looking at it, by not looking out the window, by looking at the instrument alone, you can decide where you are, what the attitude of the aircraft is, whether you are turning left or right. None of this was available[26] to them. But Fitzmaurice and Köhl had taken great care to practise the art of blind flying, so they were not new to the skill of flying through cloud.

JAMES FITZMAURICE: We were lost for a long number of hours in the air at night, in cloud. We were picking up ice and running out of oil which is very important with a little motor of that sort. We had just a 300 horse power engine. Then the compass and some of our other instruments failed to work. Still we were able to work out our position by the stars whenever we saw them.

Meanwhile back in Germany and Ireland the families and friends of the three men sat waiting for news. May Fitzmaurice remembers the tension at the time:

---

22 *indicator* – Anzeiger, Messer, Tafel
23 *altimeter* – Höhenmesser
24 *attitude* – Lage
25 *artificial horizon* – künstlicher Horizont
26 *available* – verfügbar

MAY FITZMAURICE: All the time I was praying for him. I felt he'd get there but you just can't be sure, can you?

But little by little they neared their destination. They had now been travelling so long that they knew land could not be far away.

April 13, 1928, 12.00 p.m.: Somewhere near the coast of Newfoundland the pilots mistake their position a number of times. Eventually, after 36.5 hours in the air and with fuel and oil fast running out, Fitzmaurice spots Greenly Island lighthouse. Greenly Island they know lies between Labrador and Newfoundland. Then at last the great moment arrived:

JAMES FITZMAURICE: I saw a light and certain signs of human life. This was our best chance.

They decide to land, hoping they are where they think they are. Köhl brings the plane down. One wheel however crashes through the ice. Parts of the plane are badly damaged. It is 1,800 km north of New York, their planned destination[27]. Nevertheless the first East to West transatlantic crossing is complete. The Bremen and its crew have made it; by the skin of their teeth.

***

As one would expect in the United States, the three crewmen were given a hero's welcome. They were taken in procession through the streets. In New York, Fifth Avenue was lined with thousands of people to watch the procession. The Atlantic Flyers, as they were called, were presented[28] with the Congressional Medal of Honor. In Springfield, Illinois they dropped a flag from the plane to honour Abraham

27 *destination* – Ziel
28 *to present* – überreichen

Lincoln's birthplace. In Chicago 100,000 people gathered at the Soldiers Field Stadium to pay tribute to the men.

Bremen, 19, June, 1928: Thousands line the streets of Bremen to welcome the heroes home.

The last word belongs to Johnny Maher. He has one special memory of those last few moments before take-off: "They forgot nothing. Every detail was seen to. They even looked at pencils and writing pads. They just took thin pads, paper is heavy. At one stage von Hünefeld told to us to start peeling[29] the bananas and oranges. I asked him if we wanted to eat them now. "Do you not want some for the trip?", someone said. Then he explained the fruit had to be peeled to save weight. So there we were; shortly before take-off, peeling oranges and bananas as fast as we could. That's how serious the whole business was. Yet it had a funny side to it as well. Whenever anyone asks me why the Bremen made to America I say because we remembered to peel the oranges and bananas! And they look at me with a puzzled[30] look as if to say "Are you mad or what?"

29 *to peel* – schälen
30 *puzzled* – verdutzt

The Forbidden Room

Many years ago on an island off the west coast of Ireland there lived a poor farmer who had three daughters. The two eldest daughters were so beautiful that all the islanders said they would both surely marry princes one day. With hair as dark as the raven[1] and lips as red as the rose they turned the heads of all the young men who saw them. These two daughters spent a great deal of time talking about the kind of man they would like to marry, the land he would have to own, the ships he would have to sail and the rings he would have to buy in order to win their affection[2].

The third and youngest daughter was by no means as beautiful as her sisters though she was pretty in her own way. Her hair was curly[3], her eyes had a warm smile and she seldom had a bad word to say about anyone. She was good to her father and did many of the hardest chores[4] around the house. Though he would never admit it she was the apple of his eye. Now the farmer owned nothing but a small garden where he grew the island's finest cabbages and each year he would row across to the mainland and sell them. With the money he made he was able to feed and dress his daughters and buy things they needed like tea to drink, tobacco for his pipe, combs for their hair and paraffin for the lamp.

---

1 *raven* – Rabe
2 *affection* – Zuneigung, Liebe
3 *curly* – lockig
4 *chores* – Hausarbeit

***

One stormy winter's night a beast[5] that lived on the Black Rock way out on the ocean came to the farmer's garden and stole some of his cabbages. The following evening the farmer sent his eldest daughter out to guard the garden. In the course of the night the beast returned and lifting her up with his two fierce[6] horns he carried her off to his home on the Black Rock. There he handed her the keys of the house saying:

"You may eat what you like, sleep where you like and do what you like until I return." Then pointing to one particular door he said "But on no account are you to go into the room behind this door".

And with that he left.

After a while the daughter noticed a green cat perched[7] on a stool. While the daughter was preparing a meal in the kitchen the cat came and playfully rubbed[8] against her legs. Then when the girl was eating the meal the cat climbed up beside her and gazed[9] with hungry eyes at the food on the table. Now whether it was because she didn't like cats or was beside herself with fear[10] we do not know but all of a sudden the daughter beat the cat away and let it go hungry. After her meal she noticed the door and wondered what could be behind it. And the more she gazed the more she longed to know what could be behind the door. When, at last, her curiosity got the better of her[11] she unlocked the door to the forbidden room.

---

5 *beast* – wildes Tier
6 *fierce* – schrecklich
7 *perched* – zusammengekauert
8 *playfully rubbed* – rieb sich spielerisch an
9 *to gaze at* – jmdn. oder etwas anstarren
10 *beside herself with fear* – außer sich vor Angst
11 *curiosity got the better of her* – die Neugier überwältigte sie

To her horror the room was full of people who at first glance[12] seemed to be dead. When she looked again however the daughter could see that they were under some kind of spell. For although they were breathing they could neither speak nor move and they were white as a sheet. Just then a drop of blood splashed onto her forehead and the girl ran from the room. No matter how she tried she could not wipe it off. When the beast returned from hunting land and sea he saw the drop of blood on her forehead and knew she had disobeyed[13] him. Taking her immediately into the room, he placed her under the spell and locked her in.

***

On the following night the farmer sent out his second daughter to guard the garden and again the beast came. He took her with him over the Atlantic waves to the Black Rock and told her exactly what he had told the other girl:

"You may eat what you like, sleep where you like and do what you like until I return. But on no account are you to go into the room behind this door".

After he left, the girl did not speak to the strange green cat but prepared[14] a nice meal for herself. Like her sister had done the night before, she refused to share her meal with the cat and afterwards sat down by the fire thinking about the beast and what he might do with her. Having nobody to talk to and nothing to do she became bored after a while . Now there's a saying in English that goes "The Devil finds evil work for idle

---

12 *at first glance* – auf den ersten Blick
13 *to disobey* – nicht gehorchen
14 *to prepare* – vorbereiten

hands to do[15]" and that's exactly what happened next. The second daughter started wondering what could be inside the forbidden room and before very long her wish to know what was behind the door was stronger than her fear of the beast. She did the one thing she had been told not to do. She unlocked the door and entered the room. There, staring blindly at her, were all the ghostlike silent faces, her sister among them. Again a drop of blood splashed on her forehead and she too was unable to rub it off. She was standing in front of the mirror when the beast came in.

"I hope you made yourself at home", he asked, taking off his cloak.

"Yes I sat by the fire the whole time and played with your cat. Your fire was very warm and cosy thank you."

"Did you not make yourself a meal while I was away?" he said.

"Oh yes, yes I did", she replied, realizing she had made a mistake.

"Yet you say you were in no other room but this one?"

"In no other but this and the kitchen", she said, her heart beating loudly as the untrue words fell from her lips.

"Why do you lie to me?" he roared savagely[16]. "Am I so terrible? I can see the blood on your forehead you stupid girl."

And with that he lifted her up, placed her under the spell and locked her in the room.

***

15 *The Devil finds evil work for idle hands to do* – Müßiggang ist aller Laster Anfang

16 *savagely* – brutal

The third daughter was taken in the course of the following night. Like her sisters before her she was warned that under no circumstances[17] was she to enter the forbidden room. After the beast had left, she saw the cat and stopped to talk to it for a while. When the cat looked at her with hungry eyes she was generous[18] and shared her meal with the cat. Then she cleaned the dishes and swept the floor. Later she asked the cat to show her round the beast's home and she spent a while exploring all the rooms the cat brought her to. Then the cat took her to the door of the forbidden room. Curious[19] to find out what was inside but remembering what the beast had told her she wasn't sure what to do. Eventually[20] she decided to trust the cat and unlocked the door. She got a terrible fright when she saw her two sisters silent and white-faced and unable to move. She felt something on her forehead so she left the room and closed the door behind her. Standing in front of the mirror she saw the blood. No matter how hard she tried she could not get rid of the stain. Shaking with fear she sat down by the fire. Suddenly the cat, who was lying at her feet, jumped up into her arms. Purring[21] softly, it reached up with one of its paws and wiped the spot of blood from the girl's forehead. With that the girl fell fast asleep.

Some hours passed before the beast returned. When his eyes fell upon the girl's forehead he was, in the words of the man who told me this tale, "pleased beyond measure[22]." Immediately he was transformed[23] into a handsome prince thus breaking the magic spell which years before had turned

---

17 *under no circumstances* – unter keinen Umständen
18 *generous* – großzügig
19 *curious* – neugierig
20 *eventually* – schließlich
21 *to purre* – schnurren
22 *pleased beyond measure* – wunschlos glücklich
23 *to transform* – umgewandelt

him into a beast who could only walk on dry land under the cover of darkness. Opening the door of the forbidden room he lifted up the two sisters and brought them back to life.

He did this for all the other people inside the forbidden room and set them free. Then he took the three daughters down to a magnificent white boat with red sails and brought them safely back to their father. Tears of joy ran down the farmer's cheeks when he saw his girls arriving home. The following evening the prince sat down by the fire and asked the farmer for the hand of his youngest daughter in marriage, the girl who had freed him from the spell.

The Photograph

"So how can you tell me you're lonely
And say for you that the sun don't shine
Let me take you by the hand
And lead you through the streets of London
I'll show you something that'll make you change your mind"
Ralph McTell

Shortly after dawn the sound of the wind and soft rain knocking at my bedroom window woke me. I turned over in the bed, enjoying the feeling of warmth that clung to my body. I lay there, half-asleep, for what seemed like ages though it can't, in fact, have been any longer than fifteen minutes. My hands felt hot. The rock concert I'd covered the night before at the Wembley Arena flashed into my mind. Eventually, I stretched my bare feet out from under the duvet[1]. A cold shiver ran up the back of my legs as I stepped onto the squeaky[2] wooden floorboards. After dressing, I drew back the curtains and looked out the bedroom window. It had stopped raining. The sky was overcast and dull. In the distance I could see the dome of St Paul's. Beyond that a patch of bright horizon: there was hope of good weather yet. My Nikon lay on the dressing table beside the smaller of the two bags I use for work. I loaded a fresh roll of black and white film and pulled the door of my apartment closed behind me. Before long I was footing it across the city.

---

1 *duvet* – Federbett
2 *squeaky* – quietschend

The light was dim[3] and many cars still had their headlights on. From High Holborn into Newgate Street and then back down towards Blackfriars there was little of interest to me: a pair of drunks fighting loudly over an empty whiskey bottle, the window of an all-night cafe with two unshaven, unhappy faces staring out at another ordinary London day, that sort of thing. Nothing particularly good. Nothing with bite. Nothing that would halt you in your tracks, stop a reader turning the page, make a person eating breakfast or travelling in the Tube show one of my photos to someone else: the kind of effect that makes all press photographers proud of the work they have done.

In the office two days before, John, my editor – a grumpy[4] chap[5] but good at his job –, had described the kind of pictures he wanted. The House of Commons was due to debate the problem of the large numbers of young homeless people arriving in London from all over Britain and the paper needed something with 'a bit of bite' as he described it. My deadline was noon on Thursday. "Go down to Cardboard City," he said. "See what you can find." "Give those members of Parliament and everyone else in this city who has a roof over their heads something to think about!" So there I was prowling the streets of Central London doing what I liked best: hunting for photographs. Sometime after six-thirty the hunter got hungry so I bought a coffee and doughnut near Waterloo Bridge. I know the vendor[6] well and often stop there for a snack. The morning was starting to brighten as I turned off Waterloo Road.

---

3 *dim* – schwach, dunkel
4 *grumpy* – grantig
5 *chap* – Kerl
6 *vendor* – Verkäufer

I walked on a little. The trees either side of the street were alive with the songs of the birds. Working at this early hour has the advantage you can hear the birds much better than later in the day. It's as if the creatures know that the noise and fumes that will soon choke[7] the morning air will also be bad for their singing. So they give it all they've got early on. With every step I took I could hear all the other, less-pleasant sounds of a giant city coming to life: the banging and bolting of heavy iron doors, the beeping of taxis arriving to take people to work, boats passing up and down the Thames, merchants setting out their goods, the early morning Cockney chatter[8] of a people I have grown to admire since coming to the capital city eight years ago. After a while I arrived at a junction[9]. I could have gone left or right. As luck would have it I went right ...

It was from the top of the next street that I spotted them. The street fell gently away from me. They were lying a hundred yards away on the footpath that ran along the left-hand side of the road. A homeless young man and his loyal homeless dog! From the moment I noticed them I could see the situation had promise. They were sheltering between the stone pillars[10] of a wide doorway. The door itself was in need of a fresh coat of paint. Both the walls and the door would give me the right sort of background; cold, unwelcoming, rough. There were no window panes whose reflections I had to think about, no cars parked stupidly in front or beside them, no traffic signs that would stick their round red faces where they weren't wanted. Even the light was falling from

7 *to choke* – ersticken
8 *Cockney chatter* – schwatzen, plappern (*Cockney* – Londoner Dialekt)
9 *junction* – Kreuzung
10 *pillar* – Säule

the right angle. My instincts told me to take a closer look. I wandered on.

I would have sworn they were still asleep. The dog's black nose and white face could be seen sticking out of the sleeping bag but it never moved while I was approaching. The man, a black-haired chap of no more than twenty, was lying sideways in the bag which had a piece of brown cardboard underneath it. A newsagent's next door was just opening. The Pakistani running the place had carried out two advertisement signs and was propping[11] them against the wall either side of the shop. One of the signs, the one furthest away from me, stood right next to the sleeping bag. Stopping for a moment, the Pakistani, a small, big-bellied[12] man of about fifty years of age, looked at the sleeping 'couple', shook his bald[13] head and went back inside.

By now the dog had heard me coming. As he stirred so too did his human companion who sat up and said something I could not hear. I decided to buy an apple or orange or anything that would allow me get closer to them. In the end I handed the Pakistani some loose change for a packet of goldgrain[14]. He smiled a bright white smile and wished me a nice day. Two businessmen passing his shop stepped off the footpath and out on to the road. I stood outside the shop entrance, then crossed the road to put some paper in a litter bin. The Nikon was sitting in my right hand. My left hand held the final piece of a biscuit. When I turned to look across the road to where man and dog were now sitting the sign beside them hit me straight between the eyes: it was one of those National Lottery advertisements with the words

---

11 *propping* – an die Wand gelehnt
12 *big-bellied: belly* – Bauch
13 *bald* – kahl, Glatze
14 *goldgrain* – a type of biscuit

PLAY HERE
Around A Million Winners Every Week

in big letters above a drawing of a hand whose index finger pointed down towards the figure of one lucky, delighted person. Raising the Nikon to my eye I got that excited buzz I always get when I look through the viewfinder and discover a really good shot. The dog had noticed I was eating something. He kept staring at me. He had a lost and hungry look about him like a child standing outside a school gate whose father has forgotten to collect him. Fortunately, the man had the pet in his arms, otherwise I think the animal would have come towards me in search of food. Stroking the dog's coat, he leaned forward and whispered something in its ear. The dog never for a moment took his eyes off me. Something then caught the man's attention and he turned his head slightly to the left as if trying to spot someone in the distance. I crouched[15] down, focused, and adjusted the aperture[16]. Then I zoomed in slightly to cut out the letter box and door knocker of the door. Perfect. The mechanical snapping of my camera's shutter and motor drive shattered the stillness that had fallen around us. Three shots in all. The whole process took no longer than a second or two. The man continued stroking his dog but he too was now looking across at me. I stood up, waited for a cyclist to pass, then crossed the road towards them.

"Dog got a name?", I asked.

"Scotty."

The animal cocked his ears at the sound of his name.

"Here you are Scotty," I said feeding him from the packet of goldgrain.

---

15 *to crouch* – sich niederkauern
16 *aperture* – Blende

He demolished it almost as fast as I had taken the photos.

"I took a couple of shots" I said, glancing at the camera. "I'm with the Independent[17]. It's for a series I'm doing. You might find yourself in the newspaper tomorrow. Like a biscuit?"

"Cheers[18], mate[19]" He took one from the packet. I noticed his hands, the nails of his fingers, bitten back, the stubble[20] on his chin, his open shirt. We talked for a few moments; about the dog mainly. They had met in his hometown and the dog had come the whole way to London with him. A regular team they were. I sensed a northern accent though it was hard to pinpoint where exactly he was from. It might have been Sunderland though I couldn't be sure. He didn't want to say much about himself. The lad[21] looked as if he'd been living rough for a while.

While we talked, I tried to imagine what living rough is like; sleeping in doorways, in railway station toilets or by the docks, week in week out. I wondered about his mother, his father, his friends, the house that he left for this life on the streets. What had driven him away? Was it a case of too much screaming and shouting or days of endless silence? The dog sniffed[22] at the packet again. I fed him another biscuit. Unknown to me, at the opposite end of the road, two uniformed policemen had appeared and were walking towards us, growing ever bigger in the young man's eyes. Suddenly, and surprisingly quickly for a chap who had just woken up, he was on his feet, rolling his bed into a tight bundle. The dog barked.

---

17 *Independent* – Londoner Zeitung
18 *cheers* – danke
19 *mate* – Kumpel
20 *stubble* – Stoppeln
21 *lad* – Bursche
22 *to sniff* – schnüffeln

"Gotta go" he said, looking nervously in the direction of the two officers. I took a couple of biscuits from the packet and handed them to him:

"For Scotty", I smiled. He took them silently. Later, back in my apartment, when the last crumbs[23] spilled from my jacket pocket I would feel guilty at not having given him the whole packet.

With that they were gone, off in the direction of Waterloo Station. I returned the Nikon to its padded[24], waterproof bag and turned to leave. The two policeman were now standing at the spot where he had lain. They didn't look at all worried that he and the dog were gone. They'd run in to him again. If not tomorrow, then the day after. They walked off. After they passed me I noticed the words at the bottom of the National Lottery ad: It could be you, it said. It could be you!

23 *crumbs* – Brösel
24 *padded* – gepolstert

Beyond Reasonable Doubt

The police officers standing at the crowd barriers[1] in front of the Supreme Court[2] were keeping the peace as best they could. That was easier said than done. The crowd that day was unusually large and very loud. Every so often a demonstrator would raise an angry fist, shake it in the face of a police officer and shout "What do we want". The word "Justice" would ring out in reply. This would be followed by "When do we want it?" to which the crowd would scream out the answer "Now". It wasn't their singing and chanting[3] that caught the attention of Officer Jim Manning who was sitting in the green Pontiac[4] parked across the road from the Supreme Court. He was reading the red and white placards[5] held high by many of the demonstrators. "Life for Harry Baker" was painted across most of them in big colourful letters. One however was different. The simple logic of it caught Manning's attention – "A life for a life". The mobile phone in Manning's hand suddenly rang. Before he answered he bit his lip tightly, a habit of his when he was nervous. Novak, his partner, had a message for him.

"Jim, the Judge is coming back."

"Okay, I'll be right over. Thanks Sal."

Manning got out of his car, locked it and crossed the road towards the steps of the Supreme Court. With the chants of

---

1 *barrier* – Sperre, Schranke
2 *Supreme Court* – Oberstes Gericht
3 *chanting* – Gesang
4 *Pontiac* – besonderer Autotyp
5 *placard* – Plakat

the crowd still ringing in his ears he headed down the Main Hall towards Courtroom 17.

***

It had been very quiet the day of the murder. As a police officer in the town of Silver Spring in British Columbia most days had a nice routine of their own. There was time to say hello to people, to ask how they were, how the kids were doing at school, to check on who was away on holidays and who needed help. The usual kind of jobs had filled the early part of the morning – a cat stuck on a high roof, a bicycle accident, an illegal whiskey still[6] that had to be broken up and of course all the paperwork which Manning hated. Reports, reports, reports!

Ever since becoming a police officer Manning had worked hard on being a friend to each of the 450 people in his town. A small town, it was located in wild but very beautiful goldrush country. Marcella, his wife, and their two children were happy there and so was he. Manning had even turned down promotion[7] and a move to his home town of Prince George in order to stay in Silver Spring. The crime rate[8] was very low and the fact that people slept safely in their beds at night was something he was quietly proud of.

When the call came that afternoon to say that Frank Duggan had been found murdered in his mobile home and that a man with blood on his shirt had been seen running towards a storage trailer[9] down a lane about a mile from the

6 *whiskey still* – Destillierapparat
7 *promotion* – Beförderung
8 *crime rate* – Zahl der Verbrechen
9 *storage trailer* – großer Container zur Lagerung von Waren

scene the first thing Manning did was arrange to meet his partner Sally Novak at the trailer. Then he called the police station in Mounteagle for back-up support[10]. On his way out to the trailer the shock hit him. Frank Duggan, one of the nicest men in Silver Spring, was dead! For years Frank had chased gold in the hills just as his father and grandfathers had done. To earn a living he ran a small cafe in town. Then, when he got too old for the cafe and the dream of gold died, he did small jobs for people such as feeding their birds, bringing the mail, working as a hunter's guide and helping out whenever he could. As Manning's car drew up at the entrance to the lane a quick look in his mirror told him that Sally Novak was right behind him.

"Who is the guy, Jim?"

"Baker's his name. Harry Baker. He's been here about a month. You go round the side. I'll see if he's at home."

When Manning knocked on the door there was no reply. His second knock brought nothing but more frightening silence. He drew his gun, stepped to the side of the trailer door and gently opened it. Out of the darkness came the sound of snoring.

"This is the police! Hey, Mister, come on out here! I wanna few words with you".

Still no reply. Manning hesitated, not quite sure what he should do next. His fingers tightened round the weapon he was holding. There was something about the situation he did not like.

***

---

10 *back-up support* – Unterstützung

The clerk of the court asked all present to rise and Judge Theodore F. Simpson, a heavy man with a messy[11] bundle of papers under his arm, walked quickly into the courtroom. While the judge was adjusting[12] his microphone, Manning's mind went over the evidence[13] he had given the defence lawyer[14] a day earlier.

"What did you do then, Officer Manning?"

"I checked to see where Officer Novak was."

"And where was she?"

"She was coming round the corner of the trailer and I waited until she was straight opposite me. We were both on either side of the front door. Then I called out again but still got no reply."

"Please continue."

The lawyer was polite but not the least bit friendly. A city slicker[15]. A guy doing a job for the sake of the money and reputation he could make, nothing more. He seldom smiled, never raised his voice, only his tone would change from time to time.

"I entered the trailer. It was fairly dark because the curtains were drawn. The first thing I noticed was a packet of Sportsman cigarettes on the floor at my feet. This set alarm bells[16] ringing in my head because Frank, the dead man I mean, smoked Sportsmen cigarettes. Then I noticed the strong smell in the room."

"How would you describe this smell?"

---

11 *messy* – unordentlich
12 *to adjust* – (ein-)stellen
13 *evidence* – Aussage
14 *defence lawyer* – Verteidiger
15 *city slicker* – feiner Pinkel aus der Stadt
16 *alarm bells* – Alarmglocke

"Well the trailer hadn't been aired for a long time so the air was pretty foul[17] but there was something familiar about it which I couldn't put my finger on[18] at first. Later I realized it was the smell of blood on the shirt of the defendant[19]."

"I see, and then?"

"I walked over to the bed, real slow like, and tapped Mr Baker on the legs."

"Now, officer, would you please tell the court what you did next?"

"The man woke, I held my gun towards him and ordered him to follow me out of the trailer. Once outside I saw the blood on his shirt and I ordered Officer Novak to read him his rights. This she did and we brought Baker into town."

"Officer Manning, let me be clear about one or two things. You entered the trailer, tapped my client, Mr Baker, on the leg and ordered him out of the room. Then when you were outside, and only when outside you had another officer read the man his rights. Is that correct?"

"Yes, Sir." The lawyer raised his eyebrows.

"While she was doing that I radioed for a search warrant[20]. When we had it we found the stolen money sticking out from under the mattress."

"Very good. Two final questions, Officer. Would you please tell the court why you chose to enter the trailer in the first place?"

"We had a killer loose in the community and as far as I knew he might possibly be in that trailer. The only hard information I had was that according to the call I got in the morning a man with a bloodied shirt had been seen going

---

17 *foul* – schlecht, stinkend
18 *put my finger on* – nicht genau ausmachen
19 *defendant* – Angeklagter
20 *search warrant* – Durchsuchungsbefehl

down the lane towards the trailer. Now, I know the person who made that call and I consider her trustworthy[21]. I felt we should check it out."

"Would you say you had a reasonable case for making an arrest as you approached the trailer."

Manning paused. Looking the young, handsome, well-dressed lawyer, straight in the eyes he said:

"No, not really. I was acting on a tip-off[22] but my instincts told me it was the right thing to do."

"Your instincts?"

"Yes, my instincts."

"Do you always act according to your instincts, Officer Manning?"

"I wouldn't say always but ..."

"You could have placed the trailer under surveillance[23], could you not?"

"Yes, that would have been an option but ..."

"You could have waited for the other police officers to come. You could have, and should have, got a search warrant first."

"Yes I could but that would have given the suspect[24] ..."

"Thank you Officer that will do. No further questions. Oh, sorry, one last thing. Was there a phone in the trailer?"

"A phone?"

"Yes, you know, a telephone. The machine invented by Alexander Graham Bell!"

"No, Sir, there was no telephone present."

"Thank you Officer Manning, that will do."

---

21 *trustworthy* – vertrauenswürdig
22 *a tip-off* – Tipp, Wink
23 *surveillance* – Überwachung
24 *suspect* – Verdächtiger

***

The sound of Judge Simpson's hammer brought silence to the courtroom and put an end to Manning's recollections[25]. Looking around the courtroom he saw the packed press box[26], the overflowing[27] public gallery, the lawyers, the judge, the defendant – his head bowed –, Novak, the clerk of the court. The tension was so fierce Manning could see it on everybody's face. No matter who he looked at he read the same message in their eyes. He thought of Marcella, the kids, the people of Silver Spring, what their respect meant to him. That Baker had been tried and found guilty by a court in British Columbia meant nothing now. This was an appeal before the highest court in the land, the biggest case Manning had ever been involved in.

"Ladies and gentlemen my eight colleagues and I have had the difficult task of reaching a decision on this matter. All Canada is watching us, looking to us, and we realize the responsibility that brings. That we have not reached a unanimous verdict[28] will possibly add further controversy[29] to an already controversial case. However, this fact in no way makes our verdict any less just. I would first of all like to speak about the actions of the police on the day in question ..."

Manning *knew* what was coming. His stomach had a knot in it the size of his fist. The judge's voice was booming[30] out clearly across the courtroom. Yet to Manning it seemed it was coming and going, one minute loud and near, the next faint

---

25 *recollection* – Erinnerung
26 *press box* – Pressetribüne
27 *overflowing* – überquellend
28 *unanimous verdict* – einstimmige Entscheidung
29 *controversy* – Streit, Kontroversen
30 *to boom* – dröhnen

and distant. At the back of his mind Manning knew everything the judge was about to say. And the hurt in those words meant Manning could barely make out the individual words themselves.

"... From start to finish the police failed to protect Mr Baker's rights. The officer in question entered the trailer without a search warrant. Not only that but in tapping[31] Mr Baker on the leg he was in fact detaining[32] him and the man should have had his rights read to him immediately. The mistake was made worse by the fact that a second officer, not the arresting officer, read the man his rights. Even had Officer Manning read him his rights[33] in the trailer, there was no telephone present from which the defendant could call a lawyer. In fact it took three days before the defendant was able to phone his lawyer. It is the opinion of this court that the shirt and cigarettes found at the scene cannot, as a result of the police's actions, be entered as evidence in this case ..."

At this point a gasp[34] went round the courtroom. The judge stopped for a moment, looked up and then returned his eyes to the pages he was reading from. The journalists in the press box were scribbling[35] furiously. Manning's head could not take it all in, the anger, the verdict, the frustration.

"... Nor can Mr Baker's confession to the police in the police station in Silver Spring be used as evidence in this case.

The fact is that every individual is free and none can be convicted[36] unless a charge is proven beyond reasonable doubt[37] in the eyes of the law. If a person has not been treated

---

31 *to tapp* – klopfen
32 *detaining* – in Haft nehmen
33 *read him his rights* – jmdm. seine Rechte vorlesen
34 *gasp* – tiefer Atemzug
35 *to scribble* – kritzeln
36 *to convict* – verurteilen
37 *proven beyond reasonable doubt* – zweifelsfrei beweisen

properly by the police or if we are not certain he is guilty then he must be given the benefit of the doubt and set free. It is the opinion of this court that it is better that 100 guilty people go free than one innocent[38] person be jailed. The police must obey the rules of law. Only when in hot pursuit[39] may the police enter a suspect's house. Many people who criticize the court for making the work of the police more difficult would not like it if the police entered their house and arrested them without good reasons and a warrant. Protecting the rights of citizens is as important as making sure criminals are caught and jailed. Any price to society caused when a criminal walks free is fully justified in a free and democratic society which is governed by rule of law. We order a new trial and declare[40] Mr Baker's appeal upheld[41]."

Manning's eyes blazed[42]. Ever before the clerk of the court could ask all those present to rise, ever before the press reporters could make for the door to telephone their newsrooms, Manning was on his feet. By the time he reached the steps of the courthouse he was sweating and out-of-breath. Leaning against a pillar[43], he watched the crowd of waiting journalists and photographers surge[44] towards the figure of a small smiling man who, surrounded by lawyers, was coming out of the main door of the Supreme Court. The same man who eight months before had beaten Frank Duggan to death with an iron bar. As Sally Novak came out of the building Manning saw the hurt in her eyes too.

---

38 *innocent* – unschuldig
39 *hot pursuit* – auf einer heißen Spur
40 *to declare* – erklären
41 *appeal upheld* – der Berufung wird stattgegeben
42 *blazed* – klitzern, funkeln
43 *pillar* – Säule
44 *to surge* – zudrängen

"Don't take it personally, Jim."

"Thanks Sally, but it's hard not to after 22 years on the force."

"I know. We got what we expected, didn't we?"

"Yes we did. Look at that guy, will you? It makes me sick to think of it – they had us on trial in there, not him. Come let's get out of here."

As they turned to walk down the steps a journalist's voice rang out loud and clear above the noise of angry demonstrators, of clicking cameras, of passing traffic:

"So Mr Baker, how does it feel to be a free man?"

Sicher durch alle Klassen!

Lernerfolg durch selbstständiges Üben zu Hause! Die von Fachlehrern entwickelten Trainingsbände enthalten alle nötigen Fakten und jede Menge praxiserprobte Übungen mit schülergerechten Lösungen.

Mathematik

Mathematik 5. Klasse G8 BY .... Best.-Nr. 90005
Mathematik 5. Klasse .... Best.-Nr. 900051
Mathematik 6. Klasse G8 BY .... Best.-Nr. 900062
Mathematik 6. Klasse .... Best.-Nr. 90006
Bruchzahlen und Dezimalbrüche ... Best.-Nr. 900061
Algebra 7. Klasse .... Best.-Nr. 90011
Geometrie 7. Klasse .... Best.-Nr. 90021
Algebra 8. Klasse .... Best.-Nr. 90012
Geometrie 8. Klasse .... Best.-Nr. 90022
Lineare Gleichungssysteme .... Best.-Nr. 900122
Bayerischer Mathematik-Test
9. Klasse .... Best.-Nr. 950001
Algebra 9. Klasse .... Best.-Nr. 90013
Geometrie 9. Klasse .... Best.-Nr. 90023
Satzgruppe des Pythagoras .... Best.-Nr. 900232
Algebra 10. Klasse .... Best.-Nr. 90014
Geometrie 10. Klasse .... Best.-Nr. 90024
Potenzen und Potenzfunktionen .... Best.-Nr. 900141
Rechnen mit dem TI-83 Plus Sek. I .. Best.-Nr. 91409
Wiederholung Algebra .... Best.-Nr. 92402

Deutsch

Aufsatz 5./6. Klasse .... Best.-Nr. 90401
Grammatik und Stil 5./6. Kl. G8 BY .. Best.-Nr. 90406
Grammatik und Stil 5./6. Klasse ...... Best.-Nr. 50406
Aufsatz 7./8. Klasse .... Best.-Nr. 90403
Grammatik und Stil 7./8. Klasse ...... Best.-Nr. 90407
Deutsche Rechtschreibung
5.–10. Klasse .... Best.-Nr. 90402
Aufsatz 9./10. Klasse .... Best.-Nr. 90404
Lexikon zur Kinder- und
Jugendliteratur .... Best.-Nr. 93443

Latein

Latein I/II im 1. Lernjahr 5./7. Kl.
Latein als 1. und 2. Fremdsprache .... Best.-Nr. 90605
Latein I im 2. Lernjahr – 6. Klasse
Latein als 1. Fremdsprache .... Best.-Nr. 90606
Latein II im 2. Lernjahr
Latein als 2. Fremdsprache .... Best.-Nr. 906082
Übersetzung im 1. Lektürejahr ...... Best.-Nr. 906091
Kurzgrammatik .... Best.-Nr. 94601
Wortkunde .... Best.-Nr. 94603

Latein Lektüren

Rom und die Christen .... Best.-Nr. 260003
Die Frau im antiken Rom .... Best.-Nr. 260005
Apollonius – eine antike Soap? ...... Best.-Nr. 260006
Antike Medizin .... Best.-Nr. 260007
Petri Abaelardi:
Historia Calamitatum .... Best.-Nr. 260008

Französisch

Französisch im 2. Lernjahr .... Best.-Nr. 905503
Rechtschreibung und Diktat 1./2. Lernjahr
mit 2 CDs .... Best.-Nr. 905501
Wortschatzübung Mittelstufe .... Best.-Nr. 94510

Französisch Lektüren

Emmy Muguet/Christiane Heller-Doyère:
Sur la trace des ours et autres contes et nouvelles – Mittelstufe .... Best.-Nr. 255004
Josette Gollwitzer:
Sur les falaises de Meschers et autres contes et nouvelles – Mittelstufe .... Best.-Nr. 255003
Sibylle Treugut: *Aventure en Corse et autres contes et nouvelles* – Mittelstufe .... Best.-Nr. 255002

(Bitte blättern Sie um)

Englisch

Englisch 5. Klasse G8 BY .... Best.-Nr. 90505
Englisch 5. Klasse .... Best.-Nr. 50505
Englisch 6. Klasse .... Best.-Nr. 90506
Englisch 7. Klasse .... Best.-Nr. 90507
Englisch 8. Klasse .... Best.-Nr. 90508
Englisch 9. Klasse .... Best.-Nr. 90509
Englisch 10. Klasse .... Best.-Nr. 90510
Textproduktion 9./10. Klasse .... Best.-Nr. 90541
Englisch – Übertritt in die Oberstufe .. Best.-Nr. 82453

Englisch Leseverstehen

Leseverstehen 5. Klasse .... Best.-Nr. 90526
Leseverstehen 6. Klasse .... Best.-Nr. 90525
Leseverstehen 8. Klasse .... Best.-Nr. 90522
Leseverstehen 10. Klasse .... Best.-Nr. 90521

Englisch Rechtschreibung

Rechtschreibung und Diktat
5. Klasse mit 3 CDs .... Best.-Nr. 90531
Rechtschreibung und Diktat
6. Klasse mit CD .... Best.-Nr. 90532
Englische Rechtschreibung
9./10. Klasse .... Best.-Nr. 80453

Englisch Wortschatzübung

Wortschatzübung 5. Klasse mit CD .... Best.-Nr. 90518
Wortschatzübung 6. Klasse mit CD .... Best.-Nr. 90519
Wortschatzübung Mittelstufe .... Best.-Nr. 90520

Englisch Übersetzungen

Translation Practice 1 / ab 9. Kl. ...... Best.-Nr. 80451
Translation Practice 2 / ab 10. Kl. .... Best.-Nr. 80452

Englisch Hörverstehen

Hörverstehen 5. Klasse mit CD .... Best.-Nr. 90512
Hörverstehen 6. Klasse mit CD .... Best.-Nr. 90511
Hörverstehen 7. Klasse mit CD .... Best.-Nr. 90513
Hörverstehen 9. Klasse mit CD .... Best.-Nr. 90515
Hörverstehen 10. Klasse mit CD ...... Best.-Nr. 80457

Englisch Lektüren

Alan Cartmell: *The Adventures of Larry Lemming*
Unterstufe .... Best.-Nr. 250030
Alan Cartmell: *Harry Hegdehog*
Unterstufe .... Best.-Nr. 250032
Alan Cartmell: *A Dog Called Leo*
Unterstufe .... Best.-Nr. 250033
Alan Cartmell: *The Green Feather*
Unterstufe .... Best.-Nr. 250034
Liam Cleary: *Echoes and Other Short Stories*
Mittelstufe .... Best.-Nr. 250008
Rainer Jacob: *Abenteuergeschichten 1*
Mittelstufe .... Best.-Nr. 80454

Ratgeber für Schüler

Richtig Lernen – Tipps und Lernstrategien
Unterstufe .... Best.-Nr. 10481
Richtig Lernen – Tipps und Lernstrategien
Mittelstufe .... Best.-Nr. 10482

Natürlich führen wir noch mehr Titel für alle Schularten. Wir informieren Sie gerne!

Telefon: 0 81 61/179-0 **Internet: www.stark-verlag.de**
Telefax: 0 81 61/179-51 **E-Mail: info@stark-verlag.de**

Bestellungen bitte direkt an:
STARK Verlagsgesellschaft mbH & Co. KG
Postfach 1852 · 85318 Freising

14-V1M

STARK